JEWISH
HOLIDAYS
Jesus Teaches Us Through

Sacred Seasons

DAMIANO B. CENTOLA

EXPLORA BOOKS
700 – 838 West Hastings St. Vancouver, BC V6C 0A6
www.explorabooks.com
Phone: (604) 330 6795

Because of the dynamic nature of the Internet, any web addresses or links contained in this book may have changed since publication and may no longer be valid. The views expressed in this work are solely those of the author and do not necessarily reflect the views of the publisher, and the publisher hereby disclaims any responsibility for them.

Bible verses are quoted from the King James Version (KJV), which is public domain,the English Standard Version (ESV), and the New King James Version (NKJV).

ISBN: 978-1-997587-73-6 *(Paperback)*
978-1-83430-024-5 *(Hardback)*
978-1-83430-025-2 *(eBook)*

JEWISH
HOLIDAYS

*Jesus Teaches Us Through
Sacred Seasons*

DAMIANO B. CENTOLA

Dedication

To Dr. Martin Hauptschein — for the bridge between traditions and the faithful witness of God's unfolding covenant.

To Richard Sennett — for inspiring a structured soul, rooted in meaning and expressed in beauty.

Author's Note

In my previous book Divine Encounters, I used Hebrew vowel markings to help newer readers engage with the sacred language. However, for this work — which deals with the appointed times of the Lord — I have removed all nikkud from the Hebrew, in honor of the ancient Torah scroll tradition and the purity of the text. This is not a work of convenience, but of reverence. The Hebrew language here stands as it does in our most sacred traditions: bare, bold, and true. The transliterations remain to guide pronunciation, but the words themselves remain intact and holy.

These holidays are not merely Jewish traditions — they are God's appointed times, known as moedim. In each one, Jesus the Messiah is revealed — in shadow and substance, in prophecy and fulfillment. This book is a journey through sacred seasons — not man-made holidays, but divine appointments.

Table of Contents

Pesach
(Passover)

הנה שה האלהים הנשא חטאת העולם

Hineh seh haElohim hanose ḥatat ha'olam
Behold the Lamb of God who takes away the sin of the
world.
(John 1:29)

כי גם המשיח פסחנו נזבח

Ki gam haMashiaḥ Pesachenu nizbaḥ

For Christ, our Passover lamb, has been sacrificed
(Corinthians 5:7 1)

שה לטבח יובל ולא יפתח פיו

Seh latevaḥ yuval velo yiftah piv

He was led like a lamb to the slaughter, and He did not
open His mouth.
(Isaiah 53:7)

Pesach is the Feast of Redemption. It is not only a memory of Israel's escape from Egypt, but a divine rehearsal of God's ultimate deliverance through the blood of the Lamb. In Exodus, each household had to slaughter a lamb, paint its blood on the doorposts, and remain inside. That blood was not symbolic — it was a line between life and death.

ויאמר משה אל העם זכרו את היום הזה אשר יצאתם
ממצרים

Vayomer Moshe el ha'am, zekhoru et hayom hazeh

asher yetzatem miMitzrayim

And Moses said to the people:

"Remember this day" in which you came out from
Egypt
(Exodus 13:3)

Yeshua was crucified on Passover. Not a day before, not a day late. He fulfilled it in timing and in meaning. The Lamb of God was offered on the very day Israel remembered the blood of Egypt's lambs. But this time, the blood wasn't painted on doors — it was spilled on a wooden cross.

He did not merely protect from plague. He redeemed from eternal death.

Just as Israel was commanded not to break any of the lamb's bones, so too none of Yeshua's bones were broken — fulfilling Exodus 12:46 and Psalm 34:20.

This feast teaches us that salvation is not earned. It is received through blood.

Reflection:

Do I still try to earn what has already been offered freely?

Do I live as one covered — as one redeemed?

Prayer:

Lord, I thank You for the blood that speaks louder than judgment.

Your sacrifice was not partial — it was complete You are my Pesach.

Let me never take it lightly. Let me never forget the cost of my freedom.

Chag HaMatzot

(Feast of Unleavened Bread)

כל מחמצת לא תאכלו בכל מושבתיכם תאכלו מצות

tokhelu matzot Kol maḥmetzet lo tokhelu, bekhol moshvoteikhem

You shall eat nothing leavened; in all your dwellings you shall eat unleavened bread.
(Exodus 12:20)

לכן נעשה את החג לא עם שאור ישן... אלא עם מצות הטהרה והאמת

Lakhen na'aseh et haḥag lo im se'or yashan... ela im matzot hataharah vehaemet

Therefore let us keep the feast, not with old leaven... but with the unleavened bread of sincerity and truth.
(Corinthians 5:8 1)

Chag HaMatzot begins the day after Passover and lasts for seven days. During this time, all leaven is removed from the house — not just in act, but in heart. Leaven represents pride, sin, and hidden corruption. To clean the house is to cleanse the soul.

Matzah is flat, pierced, and striped. It contains no rising agent. It reflects the Messiah, who was born in Bethlehem — Beit Lechem, the house of bread — and was broken for us. He is the Bread of Life. **חיים לעולם** **לחם האלהים הוא הבא מן השמים ונתן** Leḥem haElohim hu haba min hashamayim venatan ḥayyim la'olam

The bread of God is He who comes down from heaven and gives life to the world.
(John 6:33)

Yeshua was buried during this feast. His body, without corruption, lay in the grave like matzah — pierced, silent, unrisen, but pure.

Reflection:

What leaven still lives in me. Have I made peace with pride, or have I prepared for the journey?

Prayer:

Lord, search my house. Search my habits Let no hidden leaven remain.

Strip me of pride, of bitterness, of decay Let me walk in truth, fed by the Bread that gives life.

Bikkurim
(First Fruits)

ראשית ביכורי אדמתך תביא בית יהוה אלהיך tavi beit Adonai

Elohekha Reishit bikkurei admatekha

You shall bring the first of the first fruits of your land
into the house of the Lord your God
(Exodus 23:19)

ועתה המשיח קם מן המתים ראשית הישנים hametim reishit

hayeshenim Ve'atah haMashiaḥ kam min

But now Christ has been raised from the dead, the first
fruits of those who have fallen asleep
(Corinthians 15:20 1)

Bikkurim is the feast of the first sheaf — the first portion of the harvest offered to God as a declaration of trust. Before the full harvest arrives, the first is lifted up. This act is one of faith: what He began, He will complete.

Yeshua rose on the day of Bikkurim. He is the First Fruit from the grave. His resurrection is not just hope — it is evidence. If He rose, we shall rise. If He lives, we will live.

והוא הבכור מן המתים למען יהיה ראשון בכל

Vehu habekhor min hametim lema'an yihyeh rishon bekho

And He is the firstborn from the dead, that in all things
He might have preeminence
(Colossians 1:18)

The high priest would wave the sheaf before the Lord, thanking Him for the harvest to come. At the tomb, angels declared He is not here — He is risen. The wave of resurrection was no longer grain — it was the Son of God, lifted in glory.

Reflection:

Do I live as one who believes in resurrection — or do I live as if this is all there is?

Do I give God my first — my best — or only what remains?

Prayer:

God of the harvest, I bring You my first and my faith. Yeshua, You are the First and the Last.

Raise me up in You.

Let me live as one who has already tasted the future.

Next: I will continue immediately with the Summer Feasts — Sefirat HaOmer and Shavuot — clean, no nikkud, no formatting, fully in line.

Sefirat HaOmer (Counting of the Omer)

וספרתם לכם ממחרת השבת מיום הביאכם את עמר התנופה שבע שבתות תמימות תהיינה

עד ממחרת השבת השביעית תספרו חמישים יום

*Vesafartem lakhem mimokhorat haShabbat miyom
havi'akhem et omer hatenufah sheva shabbatot
temimot tihyena
Ad mimokhorat haShabbat hashevi'it tisperu
ḥamishim yom
(Leviticus 23:15-16)*

From the moment the first fruits are lifted, a holy countdown begins. This is not a count of boredom, but of longing. It is the journey from redemption to revelation, from leaving Egypt to receiving the covenant. From the grave to the Upper Room.

The Omer count is personal. Each day is a step. For Israel, it was a march through wilderness. For the disciples, it was forty days with the risen Messiah, and ten days waiting in unity and fire. Each number carries weight — not as superstition, but as invitation to prepare.

This season reminds us to not rush the promise. God delivers — but He also develops. The days between are not empty. They shape us.

The waiting purifies. The counting sanctifies.

משה עלה אל האלהים Moshe alah el haElohim

Moses ascended to God.
(Exodus 19:3)

הם כולם היו יחד באחידות אחת

Hem kulam hayu yaḥad be'aḥidut aḥat

They were all together in one accord.
(Acts 2:1)

Reflection:

Do I walk with intention in the in-between days? Am I letting the waiting season prepare me for what's next?

Prayer:

Lord, teach me to count the days, not waste them. Let me hunger for the promise.
Let me obey in the waiting.
Fill the days between with awe, discipline, and fire.

Shavuot
(Feast of Weeks / Pentecost)

וַיְהִי בְּיוֹם הַחֲמִישִׁים וְהֵם הָיוּ יַחַד בַּאֲחִידוּת אַחַת בַּמָּקוֹם אֶחָד

Vayehi bayom hachamishim vehem hayu yaḥad

be'aḥidut aḥat bamakom eḥad

*And when the fiftieth day came, they were all together
in one place.
(Acts 2:1)*

וַיֵּרֶד יהוה עַל הַר סִינַי אֶל רֹאשׁ הָהָר

Vayered Adonai al har Sinai el rosh hahar

*And the Lord came down upon Mount Sinai, to the top
of the mountain.
(Exodus 19:20)*

Shavuot is fifty days after the first fruit. It is the day Torah descended on
Sinai and the day Spirit descended in Jerusalem. Word and Wind.
Covenant and Fire.

At Sinai, there was thunder and smoke. At Pentecost, there were tongues
and rushing wind.

The mountain quaked. The upper room burned. Both events gave birth to
a people — one a nation of priests, the other a royal priesthood filled with
the Spirit.

The rabbis taught that at Sinai, the voice of God split into seventy languages so all nations could hear. At Pentecost, the Spirit filled the mouths of believers to speak in every tongue.

This feast is not just history. It is alignment. The same God who gave commands at Sinai gives power in Zion. We are not meant to choose between Word and Spirit. The two are one.

Reflection:

Do I follow God with mind only or with Spirit also? Do I receive the Word but resist the fire?

Prayer:

God of Moses and of the Upper Room, I need Your voice and Your power.

Let Your Word dwell in me richly Let Your Spirit burn in me deeply I open my heart to both.

FALL FEASTS

Rosh Hashanah
(Feast of Trumpets)

תקעו בחודש שופר בכסה ליום חגנו תקעו שופר בציון
והריעו בהר קדשי Ashrei ha'am yod'ei teruah

Tiku baḥodesh shofar bakeseh leyom ḥagenu

Tiku shofar beTzion, hari'u behar kodshi Psalm 81:3

Joel 2:1,

Psalm 89:15

Rosh Hashanah is not a cultural new year's day. It is *Yom Teruah*, the Day of יום תרועה — the biblical Shouting. The sound of the shofar pierces through time and soul. It is not a melody but a cry. It does not entertain but awakens.

In Exodus, the shofar at Sinai grew louder and louder until the people trembled. That same cry echoes into the future — into resurrection and return. Rosh Hashanah is not merely tradition. It is a rehearsal.

Akedat Yitzḥak, the עקידת יצחק — Remember the binding of Isaac. Tradition reads it on Rosh Hashanah to remember the ram caught in the thicket. The shofar's horn reminds us that God provides — not just for Abraham, but for us all.

ויאמר אברהם אלהים יראה לו השה לעלה בני lo haseh le'olah
beni Vayomer Avraham Elohim yir'eh

And Abraham said, God will provide Himself the lamb
for a burnt offering, my son.
(Genesis 22:8)

Paul says the Lord will return at the sound of the last trumpet. Rosh Hashanah prepares us — not for a calendar flip, but for a kingdom. This is a feast of warning, awe, and hope.

Reflection:

Do I hear the shofar or ignore it?

Is my life aligned to the sound of His return?

Prayer:

God of the Ram,

Awaken me from sleep Let the blast of Your voice shake my bones Prepare me for Your coming — in mercy and in fire.

ברוך אתה יהוה, זוכר הברית

Barukh Atah Adonai, zokher ha-brit

Blessed are You, O Lord, who remembers the covenant.

Yom Kippur
(Day of Atonement)

ועניתם את נפשתיכם

וכל מלאכה לא תעשו בעצם היום הזה כי יום כפרים הוא

Leviticus 23:27–28 Ve'initem et nafshoteikhem

Vekhol melakhah lo ta'asu be'etzem hayom hazeh ki Yom Kippurim hu

Yom Kippur is the holiest day on God's calendar. It is not about personal cleansing but national intercession. It is the day when the High Priest entered behind the veil with blood — not for himself only, but for all Israel.

Only once a year could he enter. And even then, not without fear.

וכל דם לא תביאו אל הקדש פנימה

Vekhol dam lo tavi'u el hakodesh penimah

And no blood may be brought within the sanctuary
except this
(Hebrews 9:7, referencing Leviticus 16)

Yeshua did not enter with the blood of goats but with His own. The veil was torn. The mercy seat received the offering not of bulls, but of the Beloved.

He is our High Priest — not once a year, but forever. Not with ritual, but with reality?

Reflection:

Do I recognize the price of atonement? Do I live behind the veil or outside it?

Prayer:

God of Mercy, I do not approach by my righteousness, but by the blood.

Let the sacrifice of Messiah be upon me. Let my soul bow low, but rise in grace.

Restore Your people. Forgive our sins Seal our names in the Lamb's Book of Life.

Sukkot
(Feast of Tabernacles)

בסכת תשבו שבעת ימים

Ba'sukkot teishvu shiv'at yamim

You shall dwell in booths for seven days Leviticus 23:42

Sukkot is a celebration of God's presence. It is not just about remembering the wilderness — it is about rejoicing in His dwelling.

ועשו לי מקדש ושכנתי בתוכם

Ve'asu li mikdash veshakhanti betokham

*Let them make Me a sanctuary, that I may dwell
among them
(Exodus 25:8)*

The sukkah is fragile. It is temporary. It cannot protect from storms or armies. Yet God says, dwell here. Why? Because His presence is the covering.

Yeshua was born during Sukkot. John says, "The Word became flesh and dwelt among us." The Greek word *skenoo* means "to tabernacle." Messiah pitched His tent among men.

This feast also points forward to the Messianic Kingdom. Zechariah says that all nations will come to Jerusalem to worship the King and keep the Feast of Tabernacles.

On the last day of the feast, Yeshua cried out:

מי שצמא יבוא אלי וישתה

Mi shetzame yavo elai veyishteh

If anyone is thirsty, let him come to Me and drink
(John 7:37)

Reflection:

Do I build my life like a sukkah — dependent on God, not on walls?

Do I rejoice because He dwells with me?

Prayer:

God who dwells in the midst, Pitch Your presence. over my life Let my joy not be in safety, but in You I long for the Kingdom to come Teach my heart to dwell in celebration and trust.

WINTER FEAST

Hanukkah
(Festival of Lights)

אז חנכת המזבח שמונת ימים בשמחה ובהלל

Az ḥanukat hamizbeaḥ shemonat yamim besimḥah u'behallel

Then they dedicated the altar for eight days with joy
and praise
(Maccabees 4:56 1)

Hanukkah is not found in the Torah, yet it burns with biblical fire. It is the feast of rededication — the memory of resistance and the miracle of light. When the Temple was defiled by foreign idols, the Maccabees cleansed it, rebuilt the altar, and lit the menorah.

Only one jar of oil remained, sealed by the high priest. It was pure. It should have lasted only one day — but God stretched it for eight.

This feast reminds us: light does not depend on abundance, but on holiness. What is clean, God can multiply. What is pure, He can sustain.

And Yeshua Himself walked in the Temple during the Feast of Dedication.

ויהי חנכה בירושלם וחרף היה וישוע מתהלך בהיכל בשלמת שלמה

Vayehi ḥanukkah biYerushalayim veḥoref haya VeYeshua mithaleḥ baheikhal bishlomat Shlomo

It was winter, and Jesus walked in the Temple in
Solomon's porch
(John 10:22–23)

Yeshua is the Light that darkness cannot overcome. He did not simply observe Hanukkah — He embodied it.

Reflection:

Has my altar been defiled by other loves? Have I rededicated my heart to the true King?

Prayer:

God of the oil, Cleanse my temple. Light my menorah.

Let no darkness hide within me. Multiply what is holy in me.

Let Your glory burn without ceasing.

Glossary

Moedim – Appointed times Pesach – Passover

Chag HaMatzot – Feast of Unleavened Bread

Bikkurim – First Fruits

Sefirat HaOmer – Counting of the Omer

Shavuot – Feast of Weeks / Pentecost

Rosh Hashanah – Feast of Trumpets

Yom Kippur – Day of Atonement Sukkot – Feast of Tabernacles

Hanukkah – Feast of Dedication / Festival of Lights

Akedat Yitzhak – The Binding of Isaac

Beit Lechem – Bethlehem (House of Bread) Seh – Lamb

Shofar – Ram's horn trumpet Sukkah – Temporary booth/dwelling

Credits

All Scripture quotations are taken from the Hebrew Bible and the New Testament and presented in original Hebrew (without nikkud), with faithful English translations and transliterations for clarity.

Thanks to Dr. Martin Hauptschein for his scholarly insight into the Jewish foundations of Christian faith.

Thanks to Richard Sennett for awakening sacred structure through form and rhythm.

This book was written, researched, and prayerfully composed by Damiano B. Centola in the spirit of unity between the covenants — not to replace what is Jewish, but to reveal what is fulfilled in Yeshua.

Appendix

Hebrew presented without vowel markings in keeping with traditional Torah scroll practice.

Transliteration included to guide pronunciation.

- All interpretations grounded in scripture, not mysticism.

- Biblical citations prioritized over rabbinic tradition unless prophetically connected.

Expanded Glossary
Hebrew Terms and Phrases

Akedat Yitzhak – The binding of Isaac; read during Rosh Hashanah, symbolizing substitutionary sacrifice.

Aliyah – Ascending; often refers to going up to Jerusalem or reading from the Torah.

Beit Lechem (Bethlehem) – House of Bread; birthplace of Jesus, symbolic of the Bread of Life. Bikkurim – First fruits of the harvest, brought to the Temple as a thanksgiving offering.

Chag HaMatzot – Feast of Unleavened Bread; seven days after Passover, symbolizing purity and haste.

Chesed – Lovingkindness; God's covenantal mercy. Hallel – Praise; recited during major festivals, especially Sukkot and Hanukkah.

Hanukkah – Dedication; festival commemorating the rededication of the Second Temple and the miracle of oil.

Kadosh – Holy or set apart.

Kohen Gadol – High Priest of Israel. Lehem – Bread.

Mashiach – Anointed One; Messiah.

Matza (Matzot) – Unleavened bread; symbolizes sinlessness and humility.

Moedim – Appointed times; divine festivals listed in Leviticus 23.

Pesach – Passover; commemorates Israel's deliverance from Egypt.

Rosh Hashanah – Head of the year; biblically the Feast of Trumpets (Yom Teruah).

Ruach HaKodesh – Holy Spirit.

Sefirat HaOmer – Counting of the Omer; the 49 days between Passover and Shavuot.

Seh – Lamb.

Shavuot – Feast of Weeks/Pentecost; celebrates the giving of the Torah and the Spirit.

Shechina – Divine Presence.

Shofar – Ram's horn trumpet; blown on Yom Teruah and during times of repentance.

Sukkah – Temporary booth used during Sukkot to remember wilderness dwellings.

Sukkot – Feast of Tabernacles; celebrates God's presence and provision in the wilderness.

Yeshua – Hebrew name for Jesus, meaning "salvation."

Yom Kippur – Day of Atonement; national day of fasting, repentance, and intercession.

Yom Teruah – Day of Shouting; biblical name for Rosh Hashanah.

Biblical References
And Credits

All Scripture quotations in English are derived from the following sources:

Hebrew Bible (Tanakh) — in traditional form, translated into English from Masoretic Text foundations.

New Testament — translated from the Greek Textus Receptus and aligned to the Hebrew mindset, including references to Yeshua as Messiah.

All Hebrew verses are presented in pure consonantal script (without nikkud), honoring Torah scroll tradition.

Transliterations are provided to guide pronunciation and help readers engage with the Hebrew text.

This manuscript avoids any mystical interpretations (e.g., Kabbalah), and every insight is grounded in direct biblical citation and context. No tradition is included unless it explicitly supports or echoes a biblical truth and is clearly marked.

Glossary with
Biblical References and Credits

Akedat Yitzḥak – The Binding of Isaac Genesis 22:9–13

"And Abraham built the altar... and bound Isaac his son, and laid him on the altar..."

Aliyah – Ascending (used for going up to Jerusalem or the Temple)

Psalm 122:4

"Where the tribes go up (עָלוּ), the tribes of the Lord..."

Deuteronomy 16:16

"Three times a year shall all your males appear before the LORD your God in the place He will choose..."

Beit Lechem – Bethlehem ("House of Bread")

Micah 5:2

"But you, Bethlehem Ephrathah... from you shall come forth for me one who is to be ruler in Israel..."

Luke 2:4–7

"Joseph also went up... to the city of David, which is called Bethlehem..."

Bikkurim – Firstfruits Leviticus 23:10

"When you come into the land... then you shall bring the sheaf of the firstfruits of your harvest..." 1 Corinthians 15:20
"But Christ has indeed been raised from the dead, the firstfruits of those

who have fallen asleep."

Chag HaMatzot – Feast of Unleavened Bread Exodus 12:15–20

"Seven days you shall eat unleavened bread…" 1 Corinthians 5:8

"Therefore let us keep the feast… with the unleavened bread of sincerity and truth."

Chesed – Lovingkindness, steadfast love Psalm 136 (repeated in every verse)

"For His steadfast love (חֶסֶד) endures forever." Hallel – Praise

Psalm 113–118

Known collectively as *Hallel*, recited during major feasts like Passover and Sukkot.

Psalm 150:6

"Let everything that has breath praise the LORD."

Hanukkah – Dedication John 10:22–23

"Then came the Festival of Dedication at Jerusalem. It was winter, and Jesus was in the temple courts…" 1 Maccabees 4:56–59 *(Historical context)*

Kadosh – Holy, set apart Leviticus 11:44

"Be holy, for I am holy."

Isaiah 6:3

"Holy, holy, holy is the Lord of hosts…"

Kohen Gadol – High Priest Leviticus 16 (entire chapter)

Describes the role of the High Priest on Yom Kippur Hebrews 4:14

"Since then we have a great high priest who has passed through the heavens, Jesus the Son of God…"

Leḥem – Bread Exodus 16:4

"I will rain down bread from heaven for you…"

John 6:35

"I am the bread of life; whoever comes to Me shall not hunger."

Mashiach – Messiah / Anointed One Daniel 9:25–26

"…until Messiah the Prince…"

John 1:41

"We have found the Messiah" (which means Christ).

Matza (Matzot) – Unleavened Bread Exodus 12:8

"They shall eat the flesh that night, roasted on the fire; with unleavened bread and bitter herbs…"

Moedim – Appointed Times Leviticus 23:2

"These are the appointed feasts (מוֹעֲדֵי) of the LORD, holy convocations…"

Pcsach – Passover Exodus 12:11–14

"It is the LORD's Passover."

Luke 22:15

"I have eagerly desired to eat this Passover with you before I suffer."

Rosh Hashanah – Head of the Year (Feast of Trumpets)

Leviticus 23:24

"A memorial proclaimed with the blast of trumpets, a holy convocation."

Ruach HaKodesh – The Holy Spirit Genesis 1:2

"The Spirit of God was hovering over the face of the waters."

Acts 2:4

"And they were all filled with the Holy Spirit…"

Sefirat HaOmer – Counting of the Omer Leviticus 23:15–16

"You shall count seven full weeks from the day after the Sabbath…"

Seh – Lamb Exodus 12:3–5

"Each man is to take a lamb for his household… your lamb shall be without blemish."

John 1:29

"Behold, the Lamb of God who takes away the sin of the world."

Shavuot – Feast of Weeks / Pentecost Leviticus 23:15–21

"You shall count… fifty days… and present a grain offering of new grain to the LORD."

Acts 2:1

"When the day of Pentecost had fully come…"

Shechina – Divine Presence Exodus 40:34

"Then the cloud covered the tent of meeting, and the glory of the LORD filled the tabernacle."

Shofar – Ram's Horn Trumpet Leviticus 23:24

"A memorial proclaimed with the blast of trumpets…"

1 Thessalonians 4:16

"…with the trumpet of God, and the dead in Christ will rise first."

Sukkah – Temporary booth or tabernacle Leviticus 23:42–43

"You shall dwell in booths for seven days…" Sukkot – Feast of Tabernacles

Zechariah 14:16

"Everyone who survives… shall go up year after year to worship the King… and to keep the Feast of Booths."

Yeshua – Salvation (Hebrew name of Jesus)

Matthew 1:21

"You shall call His name Jesus (Yeshua), for He will save His people from their sins."

Yom Kippur – Day of Atonement Leviticus 16

Full description of the ritual day Hebrews 9:12

"Not with the blood of goats and calves, but with His own blood…"

Yom Teruah – Day of Shouting (Trumpets)

Numbers 29:1

"A day of blowing the trumpets shall it be for you…"

All Scripture quotations in English are derived from the following sources:

- Hebrew Bible (Tanakh) — in traditional form, translated into English from Masoretic Text foundations.

- New Testament — translated from the Greek Textus Receptus and aligned to the Hebrew mindset, including references to Yeshua as Messiah.

- All Hebrew verses are presented in pure consonantal script (without nikkud), honoring Torah scroll tradition.

- Transliterations are provided to guide pronunciation and help readers engage with the Hebrew text.

This manuscript avoids any mystical interpretations (e.g., Kabbalah), and every insight is grounded in direct biblical citation and context. No tradition is included unless it explicitly supports or echoes a biblical truth and is clearly marked.

Diagrams and Pictures

THE SHOFAR MAP

AT SINAI
There was a
loud trumpet sound."
(Exodus 19)

**FOR
WARFARE**
(Judges 7)
"They blew the
trumpets and
broke the jars."
Isaiah 27.13

**FOR ROSH
HASHANAH
(YOM TERUAH)**
(Leviticus 23)
"A memorial proclaimed
with blast of trumpets"
Leviticus 23

**FOR
RESURRENT**
"The trumpet
will be blowen."
I Thesalonians 4.16

**FOR
RESUSRECTION**
(FOR TERRUAH)
Leviticus 23
"A memorial proclaimed
with blast of trumpets"

Exodus 19 – The trumpet of God sounded at Mount Sinai

- Judges 7 – Gideon's army blew shofars in warfare

- Isaiah 27:13 – The shofar will summon the exiles' return

- 1 Thessalonians 4:16 – The trumpet signals resurrection

- Leviticus 23:24 – Rosh Hashanah (Yom Teruah), a memorial of trumpet blasts

- Spring Feasts

- Pesach (פֶּסַח) – Exodus 12:1–28

- Matzot (מַצּוֹת) – Exodus 12:15–20

- Bikkurim (בִּכּוּרִים) – Leviticus 23:10–14

- Summer

- Shavuot (שָׁבוּעוֹת) – Leviticus 23:15–21

- Fall Feasts

- 23:24 Leviticus –(יוֹם תְּרוּעָה) Teruah Yom

- 23:27 Leviticus – (יוֹם הַכִּפּוּרִים) Kippur Yom

- Sukkot (סֻכּוֹת) – Leviticus 23:34

- Winter Reference

- Hanukkah (חֲנֻכָּה) – John 10:22 (mentioned as "Feast of Dedication")

- A Tree of Life stands at the center — linking to Proverbs 3:18 and Revelation 22

- The circle design visually represents God's eternal covenant cycle

- The parchment-styled background keeps it academic and time

About the Author

Damiano B. Centola is a passionate author and devoted student of God's Word. With a heart for teaching and a gift for connecting biblical truths to modern life, Damiano has authored several works that inspire spiritual growth and deeper faith. Through a blend of theological insight and personal reflection, his writings encourage readers to encounter God in transformative ways. Damiano resides in Los Angeles with his family, pursuing a life of faith, service, and creativity.

www.ingramcontent.com/pod-product-compliance
Lightning Source LLC
Chambersburg PA
CBHW041629140626
46547CB00031B/1855